I'm Reading About

CALIFORNIA

The Golden State!

GALLOPADE

by Carole Marsh

Printed and Manufactured in Peachtree City, GA., USA
www.gallopade.com

Book design: John Hanson

Editorial manager: Janice Baker

California is a great state.

It is one of a kind.

What makes California special?

Let's read about it and see!

Who lived in California first?

Native Americans did!

They moved around to find food.
They hunted in California's woods.
They fished in California's rivers.
They gathered fruits and seeds and nuts.

EXPLORERS

The first explorers came to California in 1542.
They came from the country of Spain.

Juan Cabrillo was their leader.
He and his men were looking for cities of gold!

Spanish priests started missions in California. They wanted to spread their religion. Father Junípero Serra set up the first mission. It was near today's city of San Diego.

A mission was a place built to bring the Christian religion to the native people.

San Diego

STATEHOOD

California was the 31st state to join the United States of America!

Isn't it great,
to be a state!
I bet California
could hardly wait!

California became a state in 1850.

California
The 31st State
Here we are!

FLAG

I am the state flag.
I was adopted in 1911.

What colors am I?
I am white with a red stripe.

Look at me.
What else do you see?

I fly high over the state of California!

CALIFORNIA REPUBLIC

CAPITAL

Say hello to Sacramento,
the capital city of California!

There is an important building in Sacramento.
It is the State Capitol.
California's laws are made there!

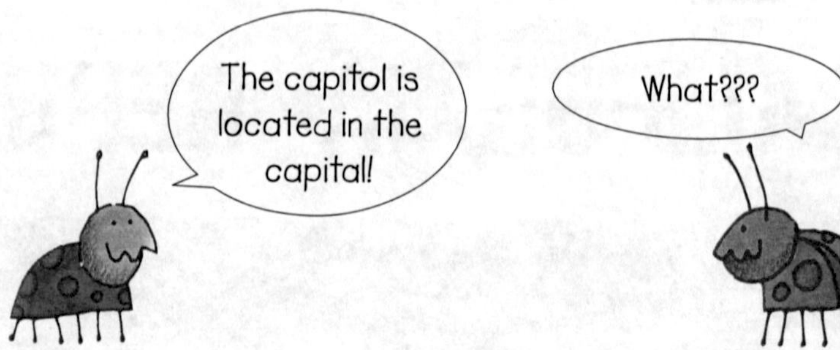

Capitol
Sacramento
Capital

SEAL

I am a seal,
but I am not the State Seal.
If I were, I would be very important.
I would be stamped on many official papers.
(Ouch, that might hurt!)

THE GREAT SEAL OF THE STATE OF
EUREKA
CALIFORNIA
Now, that's official!

NICKNAME

State nicknames are fun!
State nicknames are great!
They share fun facts
about each state!

California's nickname is "The Golden State."

Gold was discovered in California in 1848!

The Golden State

BORDERS

Look at California.
California is in a region called "the Southwest."

California borders three other states.
It also borders the country of Mexico.
Find California and its neighbors on the map!

Early explorers thought California was an island.

Borders

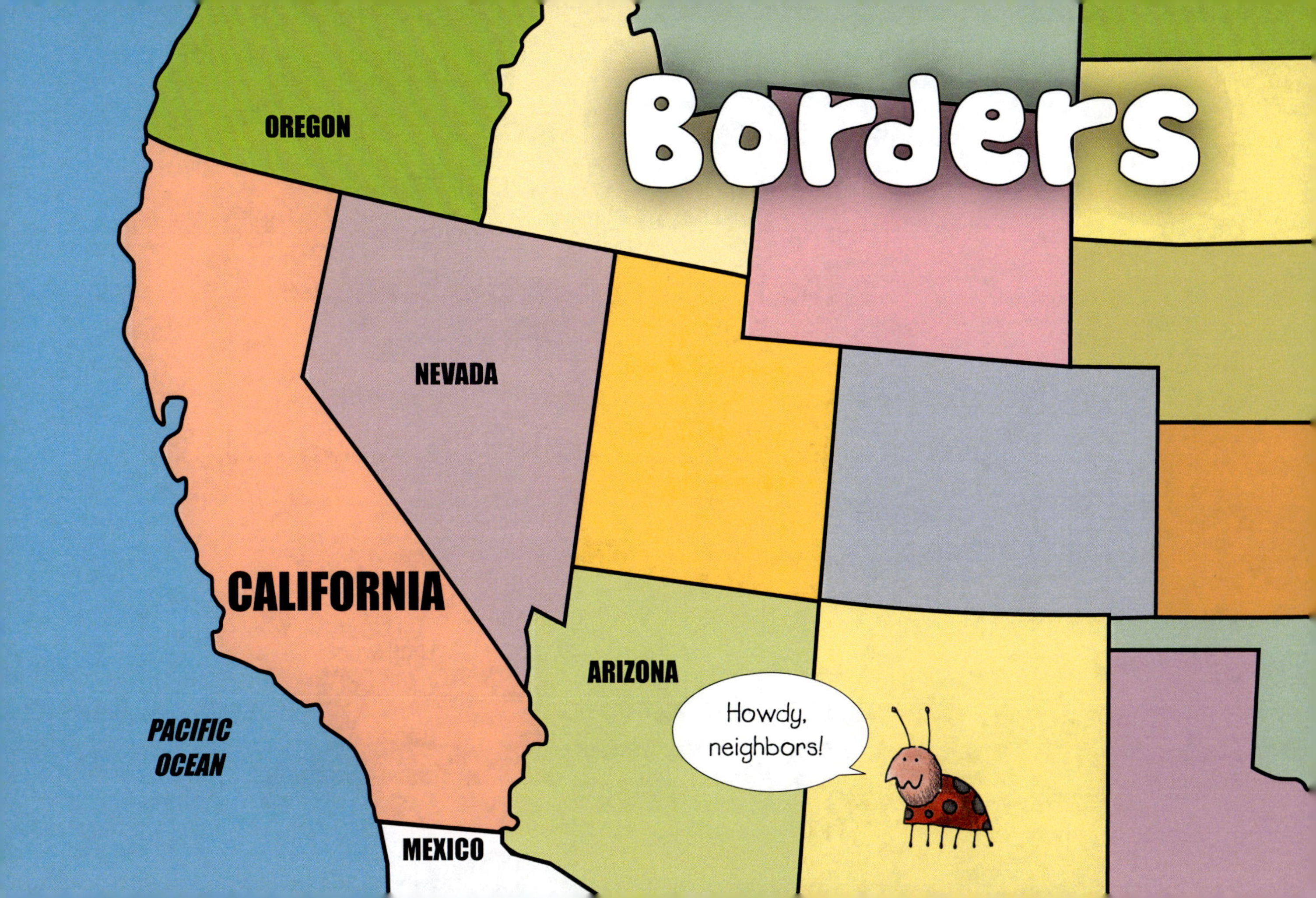
OREGON
NEVADA
CALIFORNIA
ARIZONA
PACIFIC OCEAN
MEXICO
Howdy, neighbors!

PRESIDENT

The President is the leader of our country.
He lives in Washington, D.C.
That is the capital of the United States.
The President lives in a big house
called the White House.

Several United States Presidents are from California!

Ronald Reagan
40th President

Richard Nixon
37th President

Many famous people

John C. Frémont
Army officer and explorer of the West

Biddy Mason
Former slave who became a wealthy California businesswoman

Walt Disney
Created Mickey Mouse and Disneyland

call our state home!

John Steinbeck

Author of the famous novel *The Grapes of Wrath*

Sally Ride

First American woman in space

Steve Jobs

Founded Apple Computers

Califonia Valley Quail

BIRD

I am the state bird, and I fly
over California, proud and high.

As I fly, up in the sky,
I flap my wings to tell you "Hi!"

The California state bird is
the California Valley Quail.

Golden Poppy

FLOWER

I am the Golden Poppy.
I am the state flower.

I grow where it's warm and sunny.
I bloom in spring and summer.
I help make California beautiful!

Look at me! Smell me!
When I bloom, I turn fields into
blankets of gold!

California Redwood

TREE

I am a California Redwood—I'm the state tree.
Along the coast is where to find me.

My roots run deep, they keep me strong.
My leaves stay green, all year long.

I stand up straight, big and tall.
Don't climb too high—it would hurt to fall!

California
Dogface
Butterfly

INSECT

I am the California Dogface Butterfly.
I am the state insect.

I flit and I fly from flower to flower.
I am looking for nectar to drink.

Look at my beautiful wings.
What colors do you see?

Pacific Ocean

BEACHES

Let's go to the beach!

We can swim in the waves.
We can play in the sand.

We can build a big castle
where water meets land.

California's beaches are home to many animals:

Sea Turtles **Birds** **Crabs** **Dolphins** **and More!**

Mountains

MOUNTAINS

California's mountains are the place to be.
Hiking, fishing, camping—
fun for you and me.

Winter weather brings lots of snow.
Temperatures drop to freezing and below!

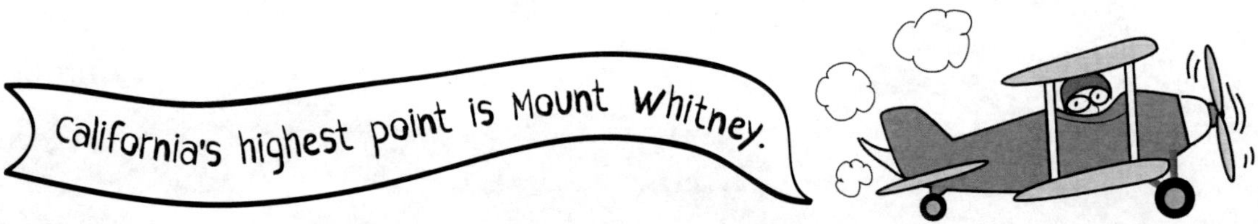

Desert

DESERT

A desert is a dry place that does not get much rain.
California deserts are very hot.
Death Valley is one of the hottest places on earth!

The desert habitat is home to many animals:

Snakes Lizards Bats Spiders Coyotes and More!

Summer temperatures often top 100 degrees in the desert!

Golden Gate Bridge

LANDMARK

The Golden Gate Bridge is in San Francisco.
It crosses the channel between
San Francisco Bay and the Pacific Ocean.
That channel is called the “Golden Gate Strait.”

The color of the bridge is
important.
It helps ships to see the bridge in
the fog!

California Crops

AGRICULTURE

California has many farms.
Why?
Because California has good soil and a warm climate!

Some of California's top crops include:

Nursery products **Grapes**

Almonds **Lettuce & Tomatoes**

Hey!
Don't forget about me!
I am a California cow.
I produce lots of milk
to make dairy products!

Sports in California

Baseball! Basketball! Football!
California has it all.

Whether you like to watch or play,
You are sure to have a ball!

Angels Dodgers Athletics Padres

Giants Raiders Chargers 49ers

Clippers Lakers

Kings

Warriors

& More!

California: Home of Hollywood

CLAIM TO FAME

The movie industry started in Hollywood, California.
Hollywood is part of the city of Los Angeles.
Many movies are made there today.
Visitors often see famous people on the streets!

Each letter in the Hollywood sign
is 45 feet high!

GLOSSARY

author: the writer of a book, article, or other text

channel: a route between two bodies of water

climate: weather conditions in an area over a long period of time

elect: to choose someone by voting

habitat: a place where plants or animals naturally live

industry: a group of businesses that provide a certain product or service

laws: rules made by the government

nectar: a sweet liquid produced by plants, especially flowers

region: an area that has similar characteristics

strait: a narrow passage of water connecting two large areas of water